This Book belongs to:

This is number 1.

Our counting has begun.

This is number 2.

Like little birds
with a Love so
True.

This is number 3.

This is number 4.

Like these little
baby
Dinosaurs.

This is number 5.

Like these bees in a hive.

This is number 6.

Like a Mother Hen with her little Chicks.

This is number 7.

Like little Angels
flying down
from Heaven.

This is number 8.

Like these Butterflies on the Garden Gate.

This is number 9.

Like these Ladybugs in a line.

This is number 10.

Like
these Pink Pigs in a Pen.

How many
Red Fruit
can you count?

How Many Trains can you count?

How many Dolls can you count?

How many Green Vegetables can you count?